Dedicated to:

Kids of Oregon.

Wherever you are and wherever you go, writing is with you.

First Paperback Edition September 2021

Authored by Joy Eggerichs Reed

Cover Design and Illustrations by Kristin McNess Moran

Illustrations Copyright © 2021 by Punchline Publishers

ISBN: 978-1-955051-04-0

Published by Punchline Publishers

punchlineagency.com

@JoyEggerichs

@PunchlineAgency

PUNCHLINE
PUBLISHERS

TABLE OF CONTENTS

Bonjour!

My name is Bernard and believe it or not, I am a talking, walking *baguette*! *(Baguette is just what you call a long skinny loaf of bread.)*

I live in Paris, France. I moved here four years ago. Do you know where that is? Lots of people like to travel here to see the beautiful buildings and eat incredible bread.

PLEASE DO NOT EAT ME!

(On warm sunny days, I get extremely hot and start to smell VERY yummy. Good thing I'm a fast runner!)

I also enjoy painting. Do you like to paint? That's another thing people like about France is all the art you can see in the museums. Many famous artists from all over the world have their paintings in French museums. I am very inspired when I go to museums. I hope one day to be as good as Leonardo daVinci.

Do you know who he was? He painted that famous lady with a funny face. Her name is Mona Lisa, and you can never quite tell if she is happy or sad.

I feel that way sometimes. I can feel both happy and sad at the same time. Or sometimes people can't tell by my face what I'm feeling inside.

What about you? How are you feeling today? It's normal and OK to feel a lot of feelings at once. Sometimes it's hard for me to say out loud what I am feeling or talk about what I need. I think Mona Lisa was probably the same way.

Do you know what else my city of Paris is famous for? Authors. *(Authors is just a special title for someone who writes a lot.)*

Many authors come to live in Paris because they think it's magical and will help them write lots and lots and lots and lots and lots and lots of words.

Personally, I think they just come for the Baguettes.

Do you want to know a secret?

You do!?

Come closer.

Closer.

In case someone is sitting next to you, I want to make sure the secret is just for you. Are you ready? Here it is…

SECRET: **LIVING** in Paris does **not** make you a better writer!!!!

BONUS SECRET: **WRITING** makes you a better writer. So the secret is all you have to do is write, and keep writing, and you can get really good at writing.

MAYBE EVEN ONE DAY YOU WILL BECOME AN AUTHOR!?!!

Sorry for the yelling, I just couldn't keep that secret to myself.

Are you ready to dive in? *(Asking if you are "ready to dive in" is just a special way of asking someone if they are ready to go. But it's kind of funny to think about isn't it? Diving IN to writing? Ha!)*

I have created three different sections for you so you can try out different styles of writing: Creative, Memoir, and Journalism. I'll tell you more about each style of writing when we get to that section.

Let's start with Creative Writing, shall we? Or as I like to call it, Imagination Station.

WELCOME TO

STATION

All aboard the train at Imagination Station, and open your eyes really wide for the ride we are about to take. Let's start by thinking about the books or movies that you like. What are some of them called? Do you have a favorite character from a book or movie? *(A character is someone or something that usually talks in a pretend story.)* If you've read the story of *The Three Little Pigs*, each of the pigs is a character, and so is the wolf!

My favorite movie, which is set in France, is Disney's *Beauty and the Beast*. Two of the characters, Belle and Gaston, are humans, but Chip and Lumiere are characters too, even though they are a teacup and a candle. They talk, sing and go on adventures just like the humans!

Now you...

My favorite character is named _____

from _____.

I would imagine that there are so many characters like Chip and Lumiere right in the room you are sitting in this moment. You just have to look really hard and use your imagination.

Follow my lead and see what appears!

LIST SEVEN THINGS YOU SEE.

(Thing = person or any object you can see.)

Here's my list from the room I'm in right now: *Your list of things you see right now:*

fork   _____
socks   _____
chair   _____
*plant   _____
water   _____
box   _____
woman   _____

Now, write your seven things inside each of the circles with three words to describe each thing. Here's one of mine:

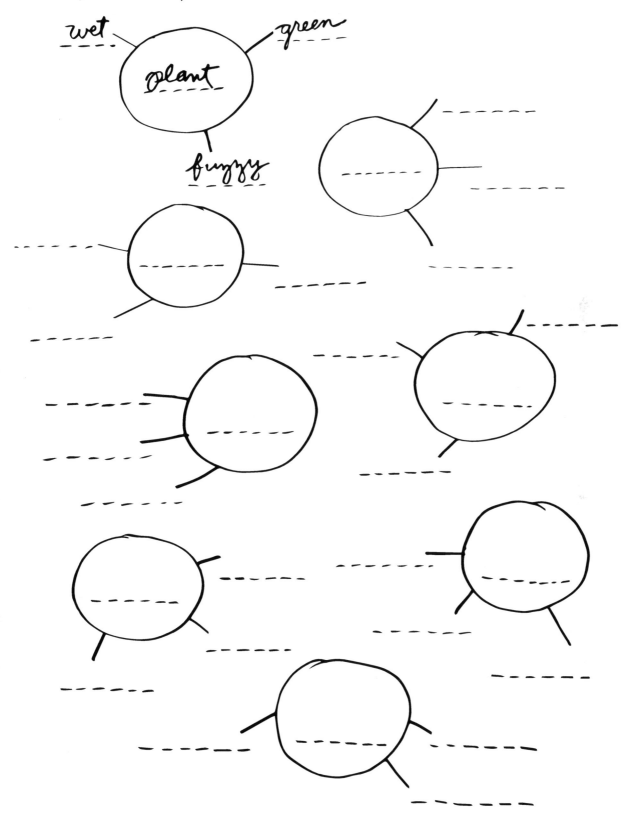

wet — plant — green — fuzzy

NEXT, ANSWER THIS QUESTION BY CIRCLING YOUR ANSWER:

Do you like to pretend? *(Pretending is when you imagine in your head that something is different than what it is in real life. For example, I'm pretending that the plant in my room can eat and talk. It loves hamburgers, french fries and talking on the phone.)*

YES   NO

If you said yes, great! We are going to pretend that something from our list of seven things could become a character in a story that you are making up!

If you said no, will you try it with me? Sometimes it's fun to be creative and make up stories in our minds!

DRAW A STAR ON YOUR LIST NEXT TO ANY OF THE THINGS IN THE ROOM THAT YOU THINK COULD BECOME A FUN OR INTERESTING CHARACTER FOR A STORY.

I drew a star next to the plant in my room. I think I could write a really interesting story about a plant who eats hamburgers.

Now give your characters names.

My plant is named Perdita.

What are the names for your characters?

If you are feeling stuck, here are a couple other character names I came up with.

The box in the room was shiny and blue. I thought about what else was shiny and and might look sort of like a box, and I thought, Ooooooh! A robot. So I created a character in my head named Robert the Robot.

There was a woman in the room and she was a little bit loud and very very tall with dark brown hair. I created a character in my head that reminded me of her. I made the character a bear and called her Barbara Bear. She's kinda scary.

YOUR CHARACTERS NAMES:

Name_____

Name_____

Name_____

NEXT, PICK A PLACE FOR YOUR CHARACTERS TO BE OR LIVE.

(Somewhere you go like school, a house you know, a city you've visited, a park you like...)

My place is MLK Park.

Your Place:_____

AFTER, PICK A TIME OF DAY FOR THE STORY TO TAKE PLACE.

(Morning? Lunchtime? Night? 8:27 in the morning?)

I'm choosing the morning for my story, because it's my favorite time of day.

Your Time:_____

Close your eyes and imagine the place you picked and the time of day. What do you see, hear, smell, taste, or feel in your imagination when you picture that place and time? Write down as many things as you can think of.

Now for the fun part! This is when your characters visit the place and time that you imagined, which sets the stage for you to write your own creative story.

Imagine two of your characters in that place you just imagined and write a story about both of them. What might they say to each other? Why are they together? How did they get to this place? Write all that down, and even if you don't know the ending, your story will begin to unfold.

Fun Tip: When a character talks, you put two little lines on either side of what they say to show that they are talking, called quotation marks. Like this...

> **Perdita The Plant:** *"I want a hamburger!"*
> **Robert the Robot:** *"I am very hot!"*

Now, you can keep building on the story you started. Close your eyes and imagine what your characters might say to each other in the place you put them. AND don't forget the possibility that another character might join them, or they might go to another place. Write everything you see in your head, and start creating your story!

Here's an example of the beginning of my story:

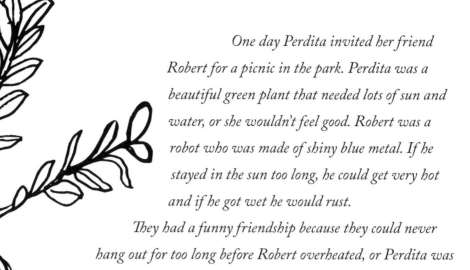

One day Perdita invited her friend Robert for a picnic in the park. Perdita was a beautiful green plant that needed lots of sun and water, or she wouldn't feel good. Robert was a robot who was made of shiny blue metal. If he stayed in the sun too long, he could get very hot and if he got wet he would rust.

They had a funny friendship because they could never hang out for too long before Robert overheated, or Perdita was too cold and thirsty.

"What a beautiful day it is here at MLK Park. I'm so glad you could join me for lunch," said Perdita.

"I agree!" said Robert, "It's beautiful, but the sun is pretty hot. We should find some shade!"

Perdita could have stayed and laid in the park all day long, but she knew that she and Robert needed to take turns playing in the sunny park, or staying cool in the shade. However, there was a question Perdita HAD to get an answer to before they left.

"Robert, I have a very important question for you."

"Sure, what is it?" said Robert, starting to get nervous.

"Are you going to finish your hamburger?!" Perdita said with a grin.

Robert laughed out loud,"Perdita, you love hamburgers more than anything in the world! Of course you can have mine. It would make me happy to share. Besides, too much ketchup makes my gears get sticky. After you finish, let's go find some shade."

"And some ice-cream!" Perdita squealed as she swallowed the last of Robert's burger and jumped up to join Robert so he could cool down in the shade.

To be continued...

That's kind of a silly story, but it's what I saw in my head when I imagined the park by my home and the two characters I had imagined. I'm not sure what happens next, but if I keep writing, I'm sure I'll discover more. That's what I think you should do too! Don't try to figure out the ending yet, just close your eyes and write what you see, then close your eyes and imagine some more. Eventually you can write at the same time you are imagining what is happening in your head, and you might even have ideas for what will happen for your ending!

I'm excited to read what you discover and learn about the walking, talking, exciting characters that were in this room the whole time.

HAVE FUN!

2

Have you ever had something happen to you and wanted to tell a friend the whole story? If you write enough of those stories and it becomes a book, it's called an autobiography or "memoir." Many authors write memoir books to share stories, adventures, and hard times from their life to their readers. The reason I like the word memoir is because it is from the French language and means "memory."

Get it?

When you share stories about your life with someone, you are telling them your memories. When you write down your memories, it can become a memoir! Since I'm French now, I can tell you how to say that word so you sound fancy.

Ready?

Say "Meh" like you might say, "bleh" when you don't like something. Now add another m at the end of it and say, "Mehm." You're almost there, now say the word "car" but change the c to a w and say "warrr."

Now put it all together!

Mehm-warrrr. Mehmwar. memwar. memwar. Memwar. Memwar!!

Memoir! There you go! Now the only tricky thing is that my country, France, spells things differently than how you might say them. Now that you have the sound correct, don't forget that it's spelled funny. Memoir. (Like Memory, remember?)

STEP ONE: FACTS

Alright, now that we have that word lesson out of the way, I'm ready to know more about your life and hear your stories. Sometimes when we write about our own life, it can be hard to figure out where to start, so I find the easiest thing is to list out facts about ourselves. *(Facts is just a word that means truth.)* So, what are some true things about you?

I'll go first...

> *My name is Bernard.*
> *I don't have an age because talking Baguettes are ageless!*
> *My hair color is blonde. (But it's very, very, very short.)*
> *My eye color is brown. (I had to run to the bathroom to look in a mirror!)*
> *Right now I am wearing a beret (a special French hat), a scarf and black*
> *round glasses. (I have very bad eye-sight. If I don't have my glasses, I'll run*
> *into a tree. (Which is actually kind of funny.)*

Now you...

My name is _____.

I am _____ years old.

My eye color is _____.

Right now I am wearing _____

_____.

STEP TWO: FEELINGS

Now I want you to write a list of all the things, people and places that make you feel happy and excited, or even make you laugh.

I'll go first...

Croissants (fancy bread)
My friend Matthew
Playgrounds
My neighbor Millie
Buses
My classmate Emerson
PIZZA! (France is very close to Italy, where pizza was created, so we have great pizza here!)
Paris
My sister Charlie
Funny TV shows
Balloons
Lakes and swimming

Now you....

Next, can you also make a list of the things, people, and places that make you feel sad or afraid, or even cry? (Sometimes the same things can be on both lists.)

I'll go first...

> *The dark*
> *The doctors office*
> *BEARS!!*
> *Falling and getting hurt*
> *My teacher (sometimes)*
> *When someone forgets my birthday*
> *My sister Charlie*
> *Seeing other people cry or angry*
> *Tests*
> *Being alone*

Now you...

You are doing great! Let's keep going. Do your best to fill in the blank parts of the next sentences to explain when you felt those different feelings, and why!

Yesterday morning I felt _____

because _____.

Yesterday afternoon I felt _____

because _____.

Today I feel _____

because _____.

These faces always help me find a word to match my feelings.

| Happy | Sad | Worried | Scared | Confused | Silly | Excited |

STEP THREE: FRAMEWORK

(A special way of saying how your story will be built or told.)

When you write stories about your life (or, a memoir, as we learned), you can write it however you want. All you need to do is write the truth. That's why we started with "facts." It's important to remember that if someone reads your story, they might not know you very well or be able to see what you look like so that's why, even though I might know I have short short short blonde hair and brown eyes, it's helpful if I describe those facts somewhere in my story. It helps paint a picture in the mind of the reader.

AND YOU KNOW I LOVE TO PAINT!!

So, what will the framework of your memoir be? Will you start by describing the city you live in? What you look like? Your favorite place to go? What happened when you were sad? A story about a time you were really happy?

Or you could start with the story of the time you laughed the hardest! I always love stories that start with something funny.

WRITE A STORY FOR YOUR MEMOIR HERE:

As I've said before, this is just a place for you to start. You have space in this book to write one or two stories about yourself, but that doesn't mean you should stop writing when you finish working on this book we've written together. You can write stories about when you were little or you can write stories about something that happened to you an hour ago, or you can write about what is happening right now!

There are so many options for you as a writer. Almost as many options as there are different kinds of desserts in France. And trust me, there are A LOT of desserts in France. Hey, I could probably write a book about that!

What do you think?! Would you read a book about dessert?

That would actually be a perfect topic for our last and final style of writing which I like to call,

3

QUESTIONS, QUESTIONS, QUESTIONS!

Have you ever met someone who is a journalist? That means they write the news we read in newspapers or watch on TV. Journalists collect facts (what we talked about in the last section) and put together a story that will help people understand an event or something happening in the world better. When journalists write a story to share in a newspaper or on a website, it's called an article. We'll end this section by writing our own articles about something we want to investigate. *(Investigate means examining the facts that have been collected.)*

Do you know HOW journalists write these stories?

You do?!

Correct! By asking questions.

Are you a curious person? Are you curious about the word curious? Ha! I was too. It means "eager to know or learn something." Eager is also a fun word. It means "strongly wanting to do or have something." If you're curious, it means you really want to learn about a lot of different things, and ask questions so you can figure them out!

Have you ever felt EAGER for your birthday to come? Eager for the first day of school so you could see your friends or make new ones?

Speaking of friends, when I moved to Paris, it was very hard to make new friends because people in Paris speak a different language. I speak English, but people in Paris speak French. Do you know why? Because Paris is in the country of France and different countries speak different languages.

So guess what I do to make friends with the people in Paris?

I SMILE!

Smiling is a language everyone understands. Some people don't smile back, which can make me sad sometimes, but many people do smile back! The next thing I do is ask that person a question, because I'm curious!

The question I ask is, "Est-ce que vous parlez anglais?"

Those words look funny, don't they? That's because they are in French. I have learned how to ask that question because it translates *(translates means you'll explain what you mean in one language in another language)* to this:

"Do you speak English?"

If they don't speak English then they shake their head "no." If they do speak English they might say, "oui!" Which translates in English to, "yes!"

Then, they speak to me in English and sometimes we become friends. Many of the friends I have I would have never made if I hadn't first smiled or asked a question.

If you are someone that is curious and likes to ask questions, then you will LOVE being a journalist.

SO, WHAT ARE SOME THINGS YOU ARE CURIOUS ABOUT?

I'll go first...

> *Books*
> *Cheese*
> *Fashion*
> *Bicycles ("Velo" is the word for Bike in French)*
> *Painting*
> *Movies*
> *Comedy*
> *PIZZA! (But you already know that...)*
> *European History*
> *How to make friends*
> *French meals*

Now you....

As I mentioned in my list, I've been curious about how to make friends, and one of the things I've learned is that asking certain types of questions is a way that can help you make friends or be a good friend to the ones you have.

Here are a few questions that you could try:

> *"Hi, My name is _____, what's your name?"*
> *"I love playing _____, do you want to play with me?*
> *"What's your favorite book or TV show? Who is your favorite character and why?*
> *"Are you okay? What happened? Would you like me to sit here with you?"*
> *"Can I help you with _____?"*

Now that you are getting good at asking questions to make friends, I want you to pretend you are a journalist working for the news. You need to write about something happening in the world by investigating and finding out information so you can tell other people.

Are you ready to be a journalist?

The first step is to pick one of the things from your "curious" list and find out facts by asking a series of questions that many journalists ask every time they are writing a story. Those questions usually start with the following words:

WHO? WHAT? WHERE? WHEN? WHY? HOW?

So then we start gathering information by finding answers to the questions.

I'll go first...

I am curious about French meals.

By using the journalism prompt questions, it helps me gather more facts and information.

 **WHO EATS FRENCH MEALS?**

French people.

 **WHAT TYPES OF FOOD DO THEY EAT?**

Bread, wine, cheese, RABBIT! and SNAILS! And something called SWEET-BREAD that is not sweet OR a BREAD. I do NOT recommend it. Trust me.

 **WHERE DO THEY EAT?**

Most French people value having meals together. They have very very long meals. The most common places are at home, a restaurant or a picnic in the park. At restaurants, many french people like to eat on a "terrace" which is a special way of saying, outside.

 **WHEN DO THEY EAT?**

Lunch is often the biggest meal of the day. They don't eat much for breakfast. If they do have breakfast, maybe an espresso *(which is just a really small coffee)* and a small piece of bread with jam or a croissant. Most people eat lunch right at 12:30 and dinner late in the evening around 7:30 or 8:30 at night.

(WHY) DO THEY EAT THIS WAY?

Meals are very important to French people so they don't eat quickly. It's a time to sit and talk and relax with friends and family. It is very important to not rush a meal with a French person, and you probably won't find many French people eating in the car or while they are walking.

(HOW) DO THEY HAVE LONG MEALS AT LUNCHTIME?

They are able to take long lunches and dinners because schools and businesses are all in agreement that a long lunch is important, so most people have a very long lunchtime every day! Another fact is that restaurants won't bring you the check to pay until you ask for it. They believe it's your right to stay as long as you want and enjoy the meal. Since everyone believes that lunchtime is a special time to meet and talk, it's easier to do!

Now it's your turn!

I am curious about _____.

DO YOUR BEST TO USE THESE PROMPTS TO FORM QUESTIONS THAT WILL HELP YOU GATHER INFORMATION, LIKE I DID ABOVE!

WHO? _____

_____

_____

WHAT?

_____

_____

_____

WHERE?

_____

_____

_____

WHEN?

_____

_____

_____

WHY?

_____

_____

_____

HOW?

_____

_____

_____

_____

An easy way to do research on what you are curious about and get your questions answered is to use the internet and ask Google. BUT, to really be a good journalist, you should have more than one resource. *(A resource is a special way of saying a place you go to get what you need!)*

Books:

If you can go to the library, the person who works there is called the Librarian and they can help you. Tell them what you are trying to learn about and they will show you good books and resources.

Documentary:

(A documentary is a film you watch that gives you tons of information.) See if you can find a documentary on the thing you are interested about and make sure you have this with you to take lots of notes as you watch.

People:

This is my favorite one! Ask other people if they know anything about what you're curious about, and if they do, ask your list of questions and as many others as you can think of and make sure you write down some of the things they say so you don't forget.

Observe:

(Observe is another way to talk about investigating but it's more of a quiet type investigating. You mostly watch and don't ask questions.) If you can sit and observe the thing you are curious about and write down what you see and notice, you'll potentially get facts that you wouldn't find in a book or documentary. It will be 100% from your own experience and observations.

Now after you have researched, asked questions, watched and taken lots and lots of notes, it's now time to write your article as a journalist. There are many ways to write an article, but if you want to write it with your opinion included, you might start with:

> *An introduction of yourself*
> *Why you're writing*
> *An exciting fact you want to make sure everyone knows*

Other useful information
End with a challenge for the reader or telling them where they can go to learn more.

Here's my article on French food!

I've lived in Paris for four years and I'm still discovering new foods. As a Baguette myself, France was obviously the place I dreamed of visiting my whole life. The French people take eating and meal times very seriously and even have laws from the government about what can and can NOT be put in baguettes. French people love their bread so much that it's also a law that even on Sunday when many stores are closed, one bakery in each neighborhood has to remain open so people can get their fresh baguettes!

France is widely known for it's amazing bread as well as desserts, wine, and bread. But, there are a few things I didn't know about before moving here that really surprised me.

If you have been in a garden or the woods, you are probably familiar with the funny looking animals we call snails. In France, they are called escargot and people eat them all the time. I almost got sick the first time I thought about putting a slimy snail in my mouth, but since I was in France, I wanted to try this beloved cuisine. I did and I could not believe it—I loved snails for dinner! Probably because they are cooked in olive oil and lots and lots of garlic. Who doesn't love garlic?

In France, they also eat rabbit that has been made into something called pate. You spread it on a cracker or bread and it is, as they say, "tres tres bonne!" (Which means, "very good!") As I have eaten my way through France these last few years, there is rarely anything I don't like. But there is one thing…

Sweetbread.

Sweetbread is neither sweet, nor bread. And I did not know this when I ordered the dish. Let me tell you about it, so if you decide to be adventurous, you know what you are getting into.

Sweetbread is the culinary name for the stomach of a lamb. I can confidently tell you, sweetbread is probably my least favorite food in the whole world. You might like it, but if you visit France, I wanted to make sure you didn't make the same mistake as me, and think it was a dessert!

Besides loving their food, French culture loves the experience of eating. They approach meals as an event and experience, not something to shove down your throat as you are driving in the car or sitting at your office desk. Meals are usually eaten at home, a restaurant terrace, or in a park.

Breakfast is very small, typically drinking an espresso, maybe some juice, and a piece of bread with jam or a croissant. Lunch is often the biggest meal of the day and most everyone eats at the same time: 12:30. You can see a restaurant completely empty at 12:15 and ask if they have a table available and they will say that they are full. 15 minutes later, every table will be filled!

Dinner is late, at 7:30 or 8 at night because people typically start their workday around 9 in the morning, take a long lunch, and leave the office around 7 in the evening.

I will leave you with a few important tips if you travel to France and want to eat out at a restaurant. These things will be very helpful for you.

1. *Make a reservation by calling ahead and saving a table.*

2. *When you arrive, say "Bonjour!" before you say anything else. (Unless it's after 5 p.m., then say "bonsoir.")*

3. *You will need to ask for the check after you are done eating and are ready to go, because French restauraunts will never want you to feel rushed.*

The French believe it is your right to stay and enjoy the meal as long as possible, and I recommend you do. And don't forget to order the escargot and dessert. Unless that "dessert" is called Sweetbread.

NOW IT'S YOUR TURN TO COMBINE ALL OF YOUR QUESTIONS, ANSWERS AND OBSERVATIONS FROM EARLIER, AND WRITE AN ARTICLE!

I hope you have had fun trying out these different types of writing. Maybe there was one type of writing you liked more than the others, or one type of writing that was harder to do. That's okay! Writers usually have a specialty, or a type of writing they mainly do, and become experts at it. Was there a type of writing you did here that you want to become an expert at?

I want you to know that I believe in you! Keep writing, and hopefully one day you can visit Paris and try an incredible baguette. JUST don't try one that is wearing glasses and a beret...

Bon Courage! (*That's French for Good Luck!*)

Bernard

BONUS WRITING SPACE!

For every copy of *Writing with Bernard the Baguette* or *Get to the Publishing Punchline* purchased, a copy of *Writing with Bernard the Baguette* will be given to a child through Every Child Oregon or a similar organization dedicated to the well-being of kids.

Inspired by:

Every Child Oregon
www.everychildoregon.org

GET TO

THE PUBLISHING PUNCHLINE

A Fun *(and slightly aggressive)* 30-Day Guide
To Get Your Book Ready For The World

By Joy Eggerichs Reed

Illustrations by Kristin McNess Moran

PUNCHLINE
PUBLISHERS

Made in United States
Orlando, FL
25 November 2021

10739079R00024